Bamboo Dreams

An Anthology of Haiku Poetry from Ireland

edited by Anatoly Kudryavitsky

Bamboo Dreams
is published by
DOGHOUSE
P.O. Box 312
Tralee G.P.O. Co. Kerry
Ireland
Tel.: +353 (0)66 7137547
e-mail: doghouse312@eircom.net
www.doghousebooks.ie

Cover image: "Bamboo Dream" by Anatoly
Kudryavitsky. Copyright © Anatoly Kudryavitsky, 2012.

ISBN 978-0-9572073-2-5

Doghouse Books acknowledge
the support from

The Irish Haiku Society

Irish Haiku Society

Further copies available at €12, postage free, from the above address,
cheques etc. payable to DOGHOUSE also PAYPAL - www.paypal.com
to doghousepaypal@eircom.net

Doghouse is a non-profit taking company, aiming to publish the best of
literary works by Irish born writers. Donations are welcome and will be
acknowledged on this page.

For our 2012 publications, many thanks to
Kerry Education Service.

KERRY
EDUCATION
SERVICE
Seirbhís Oideachais Chiarraí

Printed by Tralee Printing Works, Co. Kerry

in memory of

Stuart Lane (1932-2007)

and

Giovanni Malito (1957-2003)

Acknowledgements are due to the publishers of the following, where some of these poems first appeared: *Acorn, A Hundred Gourds, Ambrosia, Blithe Spirit, Frogpond, Haiku Presence, The Heron's Nest, Haiku Spirit, The Lace Curtain, Lishanu, Modern Haiku, Notes from the Gean, Paper Wasp, Poetry Ireland Review, Roadrunner, Shamrock, Simply Haiku, Time Haiku, Tinywords, World Haiku Review, Because of the Seagull* by Gilles Fabre (Fishing Cat Press, 2005), *Both Sides Now* by Peter Keane (Doghouse, 2004), *Capering Moons* by Anatoly Kudryavitsky (Doghouse, 2011), *Cold Moon: Erotic Haiku* by Gabriel Rosenstock (Brandon Books, 1993), *Crossings: 21 Bridges* by Tony Curtis (Design Factory, 2004), *Double Rainbow* by Maeve O'Sullivan and Kim Richardson (Alba Publishing, 2005), *Eternity Smith* by Juanita Casey (Dolmen Books, 1985), *Feeling for Infinity* by Clare McDonnell (Summer Palace Press, 2006), *Gleanings* by Cathal Ó Searcaigh (Nivala Books, 2006), *Horse by the River* by Juanita Casey (Dolmen Books, 1985), *Hundred Haiku* (Iron Press, 1991), *Inchicore Haiku* by Michael Harnett (from *Collected Poems*, Gallery Press, 2001), *Initial Response: An A-Z of haiku moments* by Maeve O'Sullivan (Alba Publishing, 2011), *Journey Backward* by Tom O'Malley (Salmon, 1998), *Morning at Mount Ring* by Anatoly Kudryavitsky (Doghouse, 2007), *The New Haiku* anthology ed. by John Barlow and Martin Lucas (Snapshot Press, 2008), *Our Shared Japan* (Dedalus, 2007), *Pilgrim Foxes* by James Norton, Seán O'Connor and Ken Jones (Pilgrim Press, 2001), *Sand Works* by Tony Curtis (Real Ireland Design, 2011), *Seeing Things* by Seamus Heaney (Faber & Faber, 1991), *Shadows Bloom/Scáthanna Faoi Bhláth* by John W. Sexton (Doghouse, 2004), *The 'O'o'a'a' Bird* by Justin Quinn (Carcanet Press, 1995), *Travelling West* by Rita Kelly (Arlen House, 2000), *Weather Permitting* by Dennis O'Driscoll (Anvil, 1999), *Whereabouts* by Mark Roper (Abbey Press / Peterloo, 2005), *Words on the Winds* by James Norton (Waning Moon Press, 1997), *Wrenboy's Carnival* by Gabriel Fitzmaurice (Wolfhound Press, 2000), *Zilvervisje Glimt Anthology* (Belgium, 2010)."In a green spring field" by Michael Hartnett is reprinted by kind permission of Estate of Michael Hartnett; "Corn-crake" by Patrick Kavanagh, by kind permission of the Trustees of the Estate of the late Katherine B. Kavanagh, through the Jonathan Williams Literary Agency.

Introduction

Haiku in Ireland

Originally nature-oriented Japanese short-form poetry that thrived since the 17th century, haiku has recently experienced colossal growth in popularity in the English language. Seamus Heaney stated in *The Guardian* of 24 November 2007 that since the times of the imagists "the haiku form and the generally Japanese effect have been a constant feature of poetry in English. The names of Basho and Issa and Buson have found their way into our discourse to the extent that we in Ireland have learnt to recognise something Japanese in the earliest lyrics of the native tradition."

In Ireland, the country with the beautiful landscape, most people are in touch with nature throughout their lives even if they don't live in a rural area. The way of living may account for the fact that the Irish people have a long tradition of appreciation of poetry and respect for poets. However the history of haiku on this island goes back only a few decades, so the development of the genre started relatively late.

The first Irish poet to write haiku as we know them was Juanita Casey. A travelling woman born in England of Irish parents, she spent a significant part of her life in Co. Galway. She started composing haiku in the late 1960s, and a few of them appeared in her collection titled *Horse by the River* (1968), followed by a few more that found their way into her 1985 collection, *Eternity Smith*. Just one example:

The pickers
have left one plum...
hey, wind

Around 1965-1967, Patrick Kavanagh wrote a single haiku, evidently not even suspecting that it was a haiku – and a worthy one! This piece appeared in *The Lace Curtain* magazine in 1971. We restore here the original version of the poem that was slightly altered in the magazine, so the first line became the title.

Corn-crake
a cry in the wilderness
of meadow

Seamus Heaney also tried his hand at haiku writing. The following piece, in a slightly different version, appeared in his 1991 collection titled *Seeing Things*:

Dangerous pavements...
But this year I face the ice
with my father's stick

In 1985, Michael Hartnett published his collection titled *Inchicore Haiku*. It comprised 87 haiku and senryu written according to the 5-7-5 format, and was the first collection of haiku and senryu by an Irish poet, so Hartnett can be regarded as a trailblazer. The poet Mark Lonergan in his essay that appeared in *Shamrock* No 15 asserted that "*Inchicore Haiku* can't serve as a model for a modern-day haiku writer. Only one of these poems passes the time's test and stands up as a perfect haiku, if a 5-7-5 English-language haiku can be perfect." He clearly referred to the following piece:

In a green spring field
a brown pony stands asleep
shod with daffodils

The 1990s witnessed more experiments in Irish haiku writing. Most of the newly-written poems were free-form haiku, even though a few poets, notably Tony Curtis and Tom O'Malley, chose to write according to the 5-7-5 form abandoned by most contemporary English-language haijin (haiku poets).

Then the era of the Internet started. Haiku poets found new platforms for creative exchanges. We should mention the strong presence of Irish poets on haiku forums, like Shiki Internet Haiku Salon, rather popular in the late 1990s, and the ever helpful World Kigo Database, where the Irish expat poet Isabelle Prondzynski has been a regular contributor. David Burleigh translated Japanese haiku into English, and his translations were later anthologised.

The first haiku magazine on the island of Ireland, *Haiku Spirit*, was founded in 1995 by James Norton. It was a print journal of haiku and related forms that published Irish and international haiku poets. All in all, twenty issues of *Haiku Spirit* appeared between 1995 and 2000. James Norton remained the sole editor until 1997 when Seán O'Connor joined him as co-editor. Quoting the English haiku poet and editor John Barlow, "borne of the Zen sensibilities of the editors, *Haiku Spirit* greatly raised awareness of haiku in Ireland and of Irish haiku internationally – not least in publishing international poets alongside Irish poets." Its demise left a void that has only been filled in recent years. Another Irish haiku magazine called *Lishanu* (http://www.lishanu.com) published its first online issue in 2005; the second followed in 2011. *Shamrock* (http://www.shamrockhaiku.webs.com), the international online magazine of the Irish Haiku Society, was founded in January 2007 as a quarterly, and has since been publishing thematic issues focusing on the haiku movements in various countries, as well as on Irish and international haiku, haibun (short prose with haiku mixed in), essays and book reviews.

Unfortunately, Ireland hasn't yet developed a culture of haiku blogging in the same way some other English-speaking countries have. The Irish haiku blogs we have seen are devoid of quality writing and display next to no knowledge of the history and artistry of the genre. One of them, ridiculously calling itself a haiku magazine, states that it "welcomes pseudohaiku as a poem in progress"!

This highlights the importance of haiku education conducted by organised groups of haiku poets. There are currently two associations of haijin on the island of Ireland: Haiku Ireland (http://www.haiku-ireland.com) founded in 2004 and launched in 2005, and the Irish Haiku Society (http://www.irishhaiku.webs.com) founded in September 2006. As things stand today, Haiku Ireland, according to their website, has thirty-three Irish poets as members, whereas the Irish Haiku Society has seventy-three. A few of the Irish haiku poets have chosen to join the British Haiku Society. Quite a number of Irish haijin are regular contributors to major international haiku magazines and anthologies; some of them have won haiku accolades in various countries, including Japan, USA, Canada, Croatia, Romania, Italy and, of course, Ireland.

Both societies conduct workshops and haiku excursions (ginko), organise haiku readings and book launches; their websites offer information about forthcoming haiku events and have guidelines for aspiring poets. The Irish Haiku Society (IHS) also holds the annual International Haiku Competition, which has become popular not only among the Irish haijin but also among the international masters of the genre.

Haiku in Ireland are being written predominantly in English, although such poets as Gabriel Rosenstock, Seán Mac Mathúna, Cathal Ó Searcaigh and Paddy Bushe created quite a number of quality haiku *as Gaeilge*, sometimes translating themselves into English. The following Irish-language haiku by Gabriel Rosenstock accompanied by his self-translation can serve as an example:

i súile an ghadhair
leis...
an fómhar

    (in the dog's eyes
    too...
    autumn)

A collection like this can't avoid raising the question if there is a distinguishable "Irishness" about haiku written by Irish authors. Indeed, should we speak of an Irish haiku tradition? One can argue that the concerns of haiku writers and the poetic devices they choose to use are similar all over the world, and have been since the times of Basho. This doesn't prevent us from customarily defining such schools of haiku writing as Japanese, American, Australian, English, French, or – dare we say it? – Celtic. And it isn't the local subject but rather the poetic traditions of the locality that matter. This determines the way the poets work with the material, not to mention that the material itself may vary a lot, as nature can be strikingly different in various parts of the world. Despite the variety of English-language haiku being written in Ireland, the Irish haiku movement is much closer to the Celtic stream than to the English one, and should be regarded as part of the former. For example, the Irish haijin often use indirect metaphors, which is rather typical of Celtic haiku –

and Japanese, of course.

Irish haiku appear more or less periodically in mainstream Irish poetry magazines, such as *Poetry Ireland Review, Cyphers* and *The SHOp*. Sometimes they find their way onto the pages of international haiku anthologies, e.g. *red moon anthologies* and *The New Haiku* edited by John Barlow and Martin Lucas. This collection, however, is the first ever Irish national anthology of haiku poetry, and features work by seventy-seven authors who have contributed to the development of haiku on the Emerald Isle. Reflecting the recent rise of haiku popularity in our country, this book offers not a compilation of poems "about" Ireland but rather the most evocative haiku written by poets born or residing here. We don't claim that we included haiku by every poet who practises the genre in this country, let alone visitors and short-term residents. However our aim was to make this anthology inclusive. We found room for a few haiku by Irish mainstream poets, as long as their texts were convincing.

With each passing month, more quality haiku are being written in Ireland, so we can foresee more haiku books and anthologies getting onto the shelves of the Irish book-shops in the not so distant future.

Anatoly Kudryavitsky
Editor of *Shamrock Haiku Journal*
Dublin

Contents

Michael Andrew

leaves falling –
old man
tunes his mandolin

chilly morning –
a scarecrow leaning
towards the greenhouse

hyacinth
in the regal flowerbed
taking a nap

spring dawn
mistle thrush's song
muffled by diesel engine

stirred from my slumber –
pine marten
stealing apples

Natalie Arkins

frosty tips of grass
crows' tails
lifted to the sky

golden afternoon
awaiting
blackthorns' adornment

Tony Bailie

rain on the window
an unfurling snail plucked
from its thrush-cracked shell

cloud streaks
scarring the sky –
hounded wind howls

frogspawn
in a sun-dried pond –
speckled mud

Pat Boran

nowhere left to hide
a lone crab scuttles between
islands of stillness

the first drops of rain
striking the limestone shelter
colour again

evening approaching
curlews stilt-walk
on their reflections

Patrick Gerard Burke

child by a tree
all the bells
on one branch

frosty morning
the long shadows
slippery

adult child –
his mother small
in a hospital bed

empty house
soft brown apples
under the tree

David Burleigh

trapped inside a pot
at the bottom of the sea
the octopus dreams

a sudden downpour
brings them to the bookshop –
schoolboys all in white

after washing up
putting a warm plate back
in the cold cupboard

hanging new curtains –
blooms already showing on
the persimmon tree

a thousand-page book
I will surely never read –
the first narcissus

the door flung back –
snow falling on the garden
in soft grey light

Sharon Burrell

lichen
a thousand lines
in the rock face

morning stillness
the beating of a bird's wings
in the snow

autumn breeze
willows paint the water
emerald green

seaside park
cherry blossom petals
billow along the path

warm rain –
lily pads surrendering
to watery graves

summer breeze –
the load of
heavy-limbed poplars

heatwave –
two lighthouses exchange
hazy flashes

cemetery –
after rain, honeyed smell
of upturned earth

a rocking chair...
two fishing boats
nodding to each other

chilly morning –
geese in formation
over the Dart line

after the storm,
skeleton of umbrella
atop a road sign

depth of winter –
a train's headlights glowing
in the half-light

Paddy Bushe

St. Patrick's Day –
not knowing any better,
lambs dance a set

the low autumn sun
crimsoning the mountain –
rutting stags roar

the moon globe
hanging on the horizon –
an unshed tear

gainéid ag tumadh
ó ghoirme go goirme
chun bualadh leo féin

> (gannets
> diving from blue to blue
> to meet themselves)
> > (*English translation: Gabriel Rosenstock*)

Andrew Caldicott

eyeing the moon
from the pipal tree,
a magpie

empty gin bottle
reflecting the flight
of geese

Juanita Casey

burning leaves...
the face once again
feels summer

the pickers
have left one plum –
hey, wind

why rage if the roof
has holes?
heaven is roof enough

under the bridge
the stream –
the leaf and I,
travellers

Patrick Chapman

cherry blossom fire
kissing the garden
to sleep

debutante flowers –
red and white skirts hitched up,
waiting for a bee

cut anthurium
planted in burnt-out kettle –
slow clock of decay

summer flowers die –
distilled into a droplet,
aphrodisiac

Marion Clarke

mid-morning shadow –
last dewdrop
rolls off the leaf

midge haze –
a dragonfly skip jives
with its reflection

low tide at noon –
in the dry rock pool
a limpet ticks

end of day starlings blinking their return

beach reading
tiny rainbows dance
on her eyelashes

wet pavement –
upon meeting we stop,
the spider and I

storm on the lough
streetlamps on Seaview
lit by sunrise

Michael Coady

ravens from the heights
throw shapes* above the belfry –
deep-croak rituals
    throw shapes: dance (Hiberno-Engl.)

Tony Curtis

under the old boat
shoals of silent fish passing –
silver in the night

this small bit of beach
puts on a new face daily –
but nobody comes

the Liffey's old song
singing softly below me
in a muddy voice

a blackbird's sweet song
lost in the wilderness of hills –
prayer for the dead

the moon on the bridge,
yellow light on the water –
first night of winter

Norman Darlington

Saint Brigid's Day –
the clank of buckets
at the holy well

neighbour's field
newborn lambs playing
in their last spring

one drop
the short journey
from cloud to ocean

grasses rustling –
a mountain wind
reaches for the sea

leaving my home town –
only the poppies wave
bye-bye

alpine pasture –
the tinkle of cowbells
in my dreams

summer dawn
the tide laps
on sandcastle walls

autumn morning –
river-mist rising
and sheep's breath

towards the hills
last light silhouettes
an old oak

after the rain:
the river
its weight

north wind –
hazelnuts roasting
on a peat fire

New Year's morning –
a single rosehip
on the withered bush

Patrick Deeley

wood's edge –
stinkhorn
lord of the flies

the leech and I
feeding each other
to the Callows river

bed of sour stones –
the river's sweethearts
all in a flap

heron holds still
a beard of minnows sways
under his chin

stoat at Cappataggle
leading six young
across the ruptured land

the apple
sun-struck where it
looks south

dead thrush on the doorstep
the cat's way
to my heart

leather-winged bat
spinning darkness
on darkness

Noel Duffy

autumn day
the toaster humming
to nothing

honeycomb –
honey and darkness stored
for the long winter

Ann Egan

wild iris flowers
yellow stars fill
a black ditch

Gilles Fabre

always first to bloom,
this cherry tree
in the graveyard

into the bowl
that survived last night's earthquake
I place my wedding ring

front door, just closed –
how long shall they be apart,
these two butterflies?

spring snow –
it has melted on all the graves
but one

everywhere,
even in my pocket,
this morning's spring wind

it has only one leg,
the seagull
that woke me up

first full moon of the year –
and it's trapped
in a bare tree!

pub's round toilet window
just big enough –
summer full moon

the pregnant cat,
more careful than ever,
crosses the street

nearly all in bloom
the poppies my neighbour planted
before she died

one last look at it –
and the gardener
cuts the rose

taking the mouse
off the trap –
how am I to die?

Gabriel Fitzmaurice

a rotting tree stump
in the middle of the woods
mushrooms with new life

Michael Gallagher

through the snow
my footprints
track me down

sudden shower
the bog stitched with
silver lamé

gentle June breeze
maple leaves
clatter

Anna Grogan

a touch of velvet
December sky
hanging low

Christmas Eve
blue lights on the trees
outline darkness

Michael Hartnett

in a green spring field
a brown pony stands asleep
shod with daffodils

Seamus Heaney

dangerous pavements...
but this year I face the ice
with my father's stick

Patrick Kavanagh

corn-crake
a cry in the wilderness
of meadow

Peter Keane

in the morning light
the mesembryanthemum
opens to the sun

dispossessed swallows
rebuilding their little lives
in another barn

Rita Kelly

bowed heads heavy
after daffodils
spelling the spring

curtains part
main act
moon in the window

dead winter
smooth sanded curves
before laburnum

Noel King

thin sky lines
spinning suns
on hospital blankets

two washing baskets
reeds loosening
by a bridge

buttercup yellow   the sheen of the sky

in the rain forest,
the whistle of
a tree fall

Sebright bantam
searching for a new lover
in wet farmyard

domestic fly
a monster on the
doll house chandelier

Matt Kirkham

hard to make out...
lambs
against frosted fields

Anatoly Kudryavitsky

bursting buds
on the bird-cherry
each one a soundless bell

tired of skywatching...
the blue sheen of
broken sea-shells

river stillness
an evening mist enters
the lock chamber

murmuring surge
mussel shells
slightly open

a grass snake
escaping into
my thought of it

discarded monuments
the afterlife
of shadows

aspen in the rain
each leaf dripping with
the sound of autumn

sheep unmoved
in the green grass...
a slow passing of clouds

frosty evening –
inside the church, stillness
and melting wax

bamboo stems –
their memories
of the sun

hazel catkins
in the mizzling rain...
a long, long dream

searchlight at the border
two halves of the
autumn sky

Stuart Lane

trees bare against sky –
the old boar in his pen
snuffs the fresh snow

ancient earthworks –
a raven echoes vanished
war cries

Leo Lavery

sewing cobwebs
in its corner –
the old Singer

woodsmoke
salty
sweet

Remembrance Day –
in Flanders the tombstones
all smartly on parade

I shut the history book
and the shooting
stops

blackbird
still peddling
its old sweet songs

local train
stopping between stations
letting the clouds catch up

lonely jogger
still leagues and leagues
from home

on the piano
dusted yesterday
dust

taking
the traffic on again –
the old tabby

the cuckoo
savouring
its one blue note

Jessie Lendennie

late August stillness
long I gaze at the pear tree
one hand on the gate

Mark Lonergan

morning mist –
the church fills
with the smells of overcoats

early Spring
her old fingers
sort flower seeds

inside the cocoon winter time

warming sun
snow glitters
then vanishes

autumn night
campfire embers flicker
at the stars

winter's evening
a wedge of geese
black out the moon

blanket of snow
the frozen shadow
of the spire

January dusk –
a camellia follows
the moon's circle

Seán Lysaght

Main Street
the bright water dances
in a wheelbarrow

Aine Mac Aodha

out of nowhere
a bee
hungry for summer

cracks in the pavement
ants pulling
a fly

spiders' patterns
on conifers...
wearing a fine shawl

Séan Mac Mathúna

maidin cheo –
an dú-chos
ag fanacht le gréin

    (foggy morning –
    maidenhair fern
    gropes for sun)

ré an fhomhair –
cad é sin a bhogann sa choill
an oíche nó a scáth

    (autumn moon –
    is that night or the trees
    that creep through the woods?)

spring lake –
a lone bird
whistles for the dawn

writing table
I watch a spoon
gather the dawn

after the storm
fog off the sea
curling into snail shells

deep in this lake
the memory
of ancient moons

busy night in the meadow –
grass leaves leaning
dew drops rolling

wet west Muskerry –
moonlight
drying the clothes

drip drip drip
eternity
also leaks

sunset pines
shadows big enough
to have their own shadows

wild geese, wild geese
sleeting through
the ebbing stars

moonlight
reducing the city
to ruins

Clare McCotter

stooping on the edge
of autumn
purple river grass

narrow lapis lake –
deeper than sky
pupil of a horse's eye

low over
rose waters
a heron

velveting the derelict roof a patch of moon

song thrush
silent under juniper –
the fog thickens

wakening
in a scullery of stars
the wino folds her home

rapeseed field the dress my mother never wore

in his black hair the bones of old prayers

May meadow at dusk –
red fox spancelled
to a frolicking shadow

bay horse entering
the clearing
entering the moon

morning rain –
weeping under birch
a mare's mane

enfolding
the fallen foxglove
a slug's soft dream

Clare McDonnell

bandaged in ivy,
last winter's
broken tree

dandelion suns
turned moons –
the wind halves and quarters them

cotoneaster
where an orchestra of bees
tunes up for summer

writing messages –
willows dip fingers into
the languid river

down the spider's thread
that ties my door,
a spark of shine

oak leaf
in a still puddle...
autumn's first footprint

Joe McFadden

"Over mountains
mountains" –
first snow

east wind –
over silent fields
October moon

Beth McFarland

laid at the feet
of a cat,
all the Alps

all the unborn children...
cherry blossom
in the wind

Iggy McGovern

waders on the shore
dancing to the beat
of the moon

Walter Daniel McGuire

autumn breeze
spider's web
convex... concave...

mid-summer sky
even the jet trails
bloom

Giovanni Malito

wide fields
basking in the sun –
a lone hare jumps

midweek rain...
slicing away mold
from the bread

lone horse
contemplating the sky –
the still pond

afternoon sun –
the butterfly landing
on its own shadow

after the rain
a sudden burst of sun
and crows

laundry day...
the snap of wind
on white fabric

over the pond,
a leaf returning
to the tree

full moon
empty
in a child's hand

mid-winter doldrums
the stone angel
with a handful of snow

low tide
the driftwood
rests

houseflies
on the window-sill
dead of winter

she's late...
snowflakes
becoming snow

Michael Massey

scattered sheep
in an early morning field –
boulders in the mist

talking it out
again
with my absent wife

Maire Morrisey-Cummins

dark November
even the gorse bush
has the lights on

icy morning –
on the doormat a snail leaves
a gift of silver

foggy day
sheep on the hills
climb into clouds

in the chair
the cat curls up
in my warmth

winter noon –
under fallen tree twigs
a mist uncurls

Joan Newmann

dead pheasant
spread for flight –
maggots celebrate

song in the heather
rising wind in the ribs of
an old piano

Kate Newmann

damp meadowsweet –
horses in mist
up to their oxters

caught in the branches
of a dead oak tree,
autumn

Colette Nic Aodha

puffs of black smoke
waft to the left and right –
fog engraves winter

James Norton

waking with a smile,
throw back the curtains –
April snow!

the little larch
still bearing its name-tag
it too turns brown

moving the slabs –
the young frogs stare up at me,
fingers spread

the window open –
moonlight fills the room
with moths' shadows

dare I tell him?
from my neighbour's dung-yard
a double rainbow

bread on the road –
first to arrive
the limping pigeon

by itself
in darkness
a garlic clove sprouts

brimful
memorial bowls
yet more rain

dinner over –
in the bowl
one grain

umbrellas:
rain from the mountain
on our drums

light almost gone:
through a swarm of midges
first star

behind the north wall
the frost lies all day:
dogwoods redden

Seán O'Connor

hot sun after rain
wet statue of the Virgin
slightly steams

riverside heron:
a glance upstream and down –
away it flies

hot day
the soles of my feet
on cold sand

arriving –
from the darkness,
the sound of crickets

steaming
after a bath
snow in the back yard

through my socks
and his old socks –
the feel of borrowed boots

4 a.m.
a neighbour I have never seen
watches the eclipse

Kamakura Bay
same smell and sound of surf
on Bull Island

late evening blue
how alone
this star

warm spring sun
a pile of dikon*
wrinkled
   * dikon (daikon): white East-Asian radish.

amongst all these blossoms
just one bud
closed

Terry O'Connor

cherry blossoms –
one more go
on the old swing

a shaft of sunlight
through the forest...
an open pine cone

a bumblebee
in summer dusk
humming along

sunlight dappling the silence of a forest trail

blustery day
a beech tree's shadow
loses its leaves

twilight
this flight of geese
to a distant bell

a misty halo
around the streetlight –
smoking hoodies

last stop
an elderly man
the only one

in a silver frame
that summer breeze
through our hair

the shape
of a homeless sleeper
graveyard twilight

moonlit
the whispers of apple blossom
to the moth

twilight...
an egret's silhouette
between worlds

Tommy Frank O'Connor

curlews curl
over the marshlands
a lament

Hugh O'Donnell

dawn
six starlings on the roof
preparing to jump

her hands
working with flour –
the cloudless sky

rainbow –
seven flavours
of rain

patter of bamboo chimes
at dawn...
wind getting up

leaf-fall –
earth's begging bowl
overflows

rainstorm –
roof leaks
water music

after last night's party, dawn chorus

leafless trees –
a one-legged man
swinging between sticks

snow
two canaries
in a covered cage

still water –
ruins lost
in their reflection

New Year's Day –
sunlight and honey
in a jar

Mary O'Donnell

foxgloves at twilight
dipping with purple secrets –
mauve sheaths drip pollen

in a fountain
downhill to the Casino,
playful ducks

Siofra O'Donovan

water rushing
through the paddy fields
morning soup

with my nose inside
a red rhododendron flower
I think of tea

picking blackberries
I catch the pale sun
in my silver bowl

on the willow path
a purple flower opens
I hurry home

moon in the sky
over the thick forest –
cry of a pipal bird

horses gallop
in the ragged field –
mice flee

an oak leans over
the river passing –
an acorn drops, unheard

geese flying south
over the mountain creek –
moon in a blue sky

Dennis O'Driscoll

the blackness of
the cemetery blackbird,
its song an octave lower

crab-apple windfalls
at the cemetery wall
no one collects for jelly

between pre-natal
and mortuary
the research unit

Padraig Ó Horgain

through leafless trees
the crescent moon –
a blackbird shatters silence

bunch of weeds
in a famine graveyard –
evening mist settles

far to the east
rise the Paps of Danu* –
smoke from morning fires

> * *two hills in Kerry named after the breasts of the ancient Irish mother goddess.*

occluded moon
in the northern sky
owl hoots

Mary O'Keeffe

November sunset
a galaxy of crows
quench the twilight

harvest moon
the playful otter tumbles
through golden shadows

distant lamp-post
a star descends onto
the tallest tree

falling chestnuts –
the thrush opens a shell
on her sandstone anvil

autumn dew
a flock of cobwebs lands
upon the furze-bush

coffee morning –
in the hull of her handbag
she stows her daughter's lunch

rambling roses –
holly berries ripen in
a pink-petalled womb

Tom O'Malley

cicadas clicking
through the hot Spanish night –
can't find even one

after rain: on my
cabbage leaves' dry stream beds,
drops of quicksilver

stiff from the iron
your cool white bed linen –
faint scent of metal

October's breath –
a powder blue mist on sloes
takes my fingerprint

the windy creaking
of this ivy-hooded sceach* –
winter's key-note
    * *sceach: a thorn bush (Hiberno-Engl.)*

Cathal Ó Searcaigh

my grandfather's scythe
rusting in the barn
harvest twilight

an ember or two glows
in the old man's ash bucket
winter morning sun

the invalid boy –
he stares at his brother
plucking a rose

Kate O'Shea

Easter parade –
friend from Ukraine
wears a black beret

low summer sky –
in the gooseberry bush
cats' eyes

lighted candles fade –
beyond the window,
flowers and people

Maeve O'Sullivan

September sunrise
seagulls strolling
across the empty pitch

summer hailstorm
on the window-ledge
an earwig escapes

behind the willow curtain
the pen builds her nest
twig by twig

her bony back
against my palm –
Mother's Day

low tide
fishermen wading
sunset on the lines

winter fog
over the river
moving with it

waxing moon –
flying across the waterfall
lone magpie

through the raindrops
through the rainbow
the opposite bank

by the stone crucifix
bursting with red berries –
cotoneaster

long ladder leaning
against a fruitless tree –
spring sunshine

Basque flower market
an orange hibiscus
trumpets its presence

a pause
in the discussion
soft summer rain

Ciarán Parkes

after rain
the sound of birds
tuning in

blackbird
holding the winter sun
in its beak

Thomas Powell

rising moon
a thrush's sudden silence
plunges dusk

communal bath –
in the blocked guttering
a row of sparrows

harvest gathering –
all around the wheat field
woodpigeons coo

countless rosehips
in October sunshine –
one red admiral

moonlit kitchen –
the stillness between
a tap's slow drips

cold winter workshop
his breath disappearing
into the day ahead

spring birdsong...
the silent fall
of late snow

broken sunshine
reaching for hazel nuts
where I grew up

turning the corner –
my pedalling shadow
overtakes

from the mist
a mute swan glides
into being

spring dawn –
a robin blazes
in the ash tree

chaffinch's call...
the intermittent drips
of melting snow

Isabelle Prondzynski

playground –
the rustling of pigeons' feet
in fallen leaves

grey day again –
the blue grape hyacinth
grows grey too

mountain brook –
a wagtail advances
stone by stone

redcurrants –
each with its own
drop of rain

chorisia* avenue –
flowers and school girls
all in pink
    * chorisia: silk-floss tree (bombax).

last rays
of the red sunset –
maize roaster's fire

fog in the city –
now I cannot see
those I do not know

sitting in silence
by the trickling fountain –
the latest ringtone

cold fog –
the balcony moss
all the greener

Christmas tree –
among sweets and tinsel
a spider's web

starlit sky –
light clouds drifting from
this year... to this...

first walk –
the freezing fog hides
the horizon

Maureen Purcell

bush trees in bloom
flying fox sucks
the nectar

cicadas
singing for a mate
soon to die

Justin Quinn

cotoneasters in winter:
unleaved they show
skeletons of sole

Mark Roper

a squashed crow's wing
lifts and waves
in the wake of a passing car

at my front door
nothing between me
and the full moon

Gabriel Rosenstock

foiche lá fearthainne
a glóirín
múcht

> (a wasp on a wet day
> her little voice
> smothered)

cow looks over
Caernarfon Bay
without knowing why

bóín Dé
orlach ar orlach
ag taisteal na cruinne

      (ladybird
      inch by inch
      exploring the universe)

snag breac
ólann lán a ghoib
dá íomhá féin

      (a magpie
      sipping beakfuls
      of its own image)

nothing left
but the gates –
temple of air

i súile an ghadhair
leis ...
an fómhar

      (in the dog's eyes
      too...
      autumn)

laethanta an fhómhair
míle crann
ag machnamh ar shuan

(autumn days
a thousand trees
contemplating slumber)

scamaill ag búiochán thiar
dhá phréachán aonair
ag eitilt soir

(clouds yellowing in the west
two lone crows
fly east)

barr a dhá chluas
in airde: cadhóit
ag éisteacht lena shinsir

(ears cocked
coyote listening
to his ancestors)

there must be light
where they came from –
chestnut blossoms

cobwebs in his ears
this November morning –
bust of a composer

corrán geal í
buainteoir
an pholúis

> (sickle moon
> reaping
> emptiness)

John W. Sexton

morning sun
field too small
for the horse's shadow

daffodils rot
in the vase
their shadows bloom

light over meadow
gnats illustrate my notebook
with their shadows

the fishmonger
arranges her fish
faces them seawards

thieving magpie
last slice of light
on the lawn

moon whitening
the sheets
their shadows billow

silence
pond has captured
the moon

the pungent spray
of next door's ginger tom –
camellias opening

troubled sleep
the half of the moon
I couldn't see

first snow
the garden Buddha
deeper

a good game
but shadows of crows
are too fast to catch

crows calling *more*
more
sky darkens

John Sheahan

fingernail clippings
on a black marble worktop –
the New Moon

reflected in windy water
man in the moon
wrinkled with age

bare branches –
balanced on a spider's web,
the fallen leaf

Eileen Sheehan

home village
nowhere to visit
but the graveyard

between races
boy-rowers chasing frogs
in the tall grass

pauper's graveyard
only the long grasses
have names

hard frost –
on the maple branch
moon sits it out

Breid Sibley

growing longer
after the summer rain
avenues of trees

patchwork sunrise
through the leafless trees –
red cardinals

swan song
the lake holds
the sound

Bee Smith

spider lace window
of the holiday hut...
end of season

the nerviness
of black ice –
job interview

even the cooker
needs a hot water bottle!
hoar frost this morning

teasing elderberries
from their heavy heads
jelly pan babies

Martin Vaughan

cherry blossom shower –
old dog wakes to find himself
in the pink

gorse alight!
the hillside gasping
for water

sundown –
the slag-heap disappears
by getting bigger

sunburst –
scent of wild garlic
fills the garden

empty garden
dotted with compost –
a dream of roses

too wet for birdsong –
canary yellow beet leaves
glisten in the rain

amber lit paths
littered with leaves –
days shrinking

abandoned harbour –
an old fishing net
still catching rubbish

snow garden
yellow tipped
daffodil shoots

morning dew
wet grass wipes yesterday
from my boots

trimming the laurel –
this year's bright shoots
first to go

storm warning –
jack rabbit caught in the gap
between flash and crack

Aisling White

sea storm –
in the whispering cove,
a blush of sea pinks

twilight hour –
an amber glow of
crickets' calls

beach sunrise
the fog returns
a dog's bark

October moon –
in the old oak,
a white cat's face

north wind
a dead spider adrift
of its tattered web

dawn   a snail uncurls from sleep

bonfire night
the village shopkeeper
donating apple crates

fishing boat at dusk –
gulls' cries
swirling the mast

budgie on the roof –
a caged one listens to
his song

desolate crag –
bracing the wind,
two mating gulls

so many cherry trees!
the pastel hues
of April rain

bog grasses in the evening –
a seagull
absorbs the light

Biographical Notes

Michael Andrew (Andrew Michael O'Brien) is from Westport, Co. Mayo. He published his haiku in *Shamrock*, and was a runner-up in the Mainichi Daily News Haiku Contest 2009 (Japan). He is a member of the IHS.

Natalie Arkins was born in the USA and now lives in Ennis, Co. Clare. She published her haiku in *Shamrock*, and is a member of the IHS.

Tony Bailie is a journalist from Co. Down. He has published two novels and two collections of mainstream poems, *Coill* (Lapwing, 2005) and *The Tranquillity of Stone* (Lapwing 2010). His haiku appeared in *Shamrock*. He is a member of the IHS.

Pat Boran was born in Portlaoise and lives in Dublin. He has published a dozen collections of poetry, prose and translations. His new volume of poems, *The Next Life*, is due in autumn 2012.

Patrick Gerard Burke is from Cork. He is an Anglican Priest and currently rector of Castlecomer Union of parishes in Co. Kilkenny. At the end of the 1990s, he was active on the Shiki Internet Haiku Salon website, where he published some of his haiku. Later, his haiku appeared in *Shamrock*.

David Burleigh was born in Northern Ireland, and lives in Japan. He co-translated *A Hidden Pond: Anthology of Modern Haiku* (1997, revised 2003). His most recent chapbook collection is *RC* (2009).

Sharon Burrell is from South Co. Dublin. Her haiku appeared in *World Haiku Review*, in *Shamrock* and in a few international haiku anthologies. She is a member of the Board of the IHS. She won the Capoliveri International Haiku Contest (Italy, 2008) and honourable mention in the Ito En "Oi Ocha" International Haiku Contest (Japan, 2009).

Paddy Bushe was born in Dublin and now lives in Waterville, Co. Kerry. He has published many collections of poetry, the latest being *My Lord Buddha of Carraig Eanna* (2012). In 2005, he won the Samhain / Smurfit Haiku Competition.

Andrew Caldicott is from Co. Wexford. His mainstream poems appeared in *The Stony Thursday Book, The Stinging Fly, Crannóg, Moonset, Boyne Berries* and *West47*; his haiku in *Shamrock*. He is a member of the IHS.

Juanita Casey, a travelling woman born in England of Irish parents, spent a significant part of her life in Co. Galway. She started composing haiku in the 1960s, and a few of them appeared in her 1968 collection titled *Horse by the River* (1968), as well as in her 1985 collection, *Eternity Smith*.

Patrick Chapman was born in Dublin. Poet, writer and screenwriter, he has published six poetry collections, the latest being *The Darwin Vampires* (Salmon, 2010), and a book of stories. His haiku appeared in *Shamrock*. He is a member of the IHS.

Marion Clarke is from Co. Down. She writes poetry and short stories. Her haiku have been published in *Shamrock, The Heron's Nest, Notes from the Gean* and *A Hundred Gourds*. She is a member of the IHS, and won honourable mention in the IHS International Haiku Competition 2011.

Michael Coady is a native of Co. Tipperary who has worked as a teacher, musician and writer. He has published five collections, the latest being *Going by Water* (2009). His haiku appeared in *Poetry Ireland Review*.

Tony Curtis was born in Dublin, and now lives in Balbriggan, Co. Dublin. He has published seven collections of mainstream poems, as well as *Crossings: 21 Bridges* (2004) and *Sand Works* (2011), which are collections of his haiku.

Norman Darlington lives in Co. Wexford. He was Renku Editor at the online journal *Simply Haiku* and now edits *Lishanu*, an online journal of haiku and renku. He is a member of Haiku Ireland.

Patrick Deeley is a native of Loughrea, Co. Galway. He works as a teacher in Ballyfermot (Dublin). He has published five collections of poems, the latest being *The Bones of Creation* (Dedalus, 2008), and books for young people.

Noel Duffy is a Dubliner. A fiction writer and poet, he co-edited (with Theo Dorgan) *Watching the River Flow: A Century in Irish Poetry* (Poetry Ireland, 1999) His debut collection, *In the Library of Lost Objects*, was published in 2011. His haiku appeared in *Shamrock*.

Ann Egan, was born in Co Laois and lives in Co Kildare. Her poetry books are: *Landing the Sea* (Bradshaw Books, 2003), *The Wren Women* (Black Mountain Press, 2003) and *Telling Time* (Bradshaw Books, 2012).

Gilles Fabre was born in France and lives in Ireland. He started writing haiku in the 1990s and published them in *Haiku Spirit, Presence* and *Blithe Spirit*, as well as in *The New Haiku* anthology (Snapshot Press). His collection, *Because of the Seagull* (The Fishing Cat Press), appeared in 2005. He is the editor of the Haiku Spirit site, www.haikuspirit.org (not to be confused with the haiku magazine of the same name).

Gabriel Fitzmaurice was born in Moyvane, Co. Kerry. Musician, singer, broadcaster, journalist, he worked as a teacher in Moyvane. He published many collections of his poems, as well as children's poetry and several bilingual Irish/English poetry anthologies.

Michael Gallagher was born on Achill Island, Co. Mayo, and now lives in Co. Kerry. He writes poems and short stories, and has been published in *The Doghouse Book of Ballad Poems*. He was shortlisted for the 2012 Irish Independent / Hennessy Awards. His haiku appeared in *Frogpond, Crannóg, World Haiku Review* and *Shamrock*. He edits *thefirstcut* literary e-zine, and is a member of the IHS.

Anna Grogan is from South Co. Dublin. Her haiku appeared in *Shamrock* and on the website of the IHS. She is a member of the latter.

Michael Hartnett (1941-1999) was born in Co. Limerick and lived most of his life in Dublin. He wrote in both English and Irish, and was the first Irish poet to publish a collection of haiku and senryu, *Inchicore Haiku* (1985).

Seamus Heaney was born in Co. Derry and lived in Northern Ireland and in Dublin. He was Professor of Poetry at Oxford and Professor of Rhetoric at Harvard. He has published many collections of his poems, criticism, translations, and a few essays on Japanese short-form poetry. In 1995, he won the Nobel Prize in literature.

Patrick Kavanagh (1904-1967) was a renowned poet and novelist. He wrote a single haiku that appeared in *The Lace Curtain* magazine in 1971.

Peter Keane was born in Co. Kerry, spent much of his life in England and then returned to Ireland. He was a member of the Scribblers writers group, and has published three volumes of his poems, the latest being *Both Sides Now* (Doghouse, 2004).

Rita Kelly is originally from Ballinasloe in East Co. Galway and now lives between Athy and Carlow. She has published several collections of poetry, the latest being *Travelling West* (Arlen House, 2000), as well as a book of short stories.

Noel King is a native of Tralee, Co. Kerry. He has worked as an arts administrator, a journalist, a fundraiser, and performed with The Bunratty Singers. His haiku appeared in over 50 journals including *Presence, Shamrock,* and on the IHS website. A poetry collection, *Prophesying the Past,* was published by Salmon in 2010; another, *The Stern Wave,* is forthcoming in 2013.

Matt Kirkham was born in Luton and now resides in Co. Down. His collection titled *Lost Museums* published by Lagan Press in 2006 won the Rupert and Eithne Strong Award. His haiku have been published in *Shamrock*. He is a member of the IHS.

Anatoly Kudryavitsky is a founding member and the current chairman of the IHS and editor of *Shamrock*. His haiku appeared in *Frogpond, Presence, World Haiku Review, Roadrunner, Notes from the Gean* and *The SHOp*. His collections of haiku, *Morning at Mount Ring* (2007) and *Capering Moons* (2011; short-list of the Touchstone Distinguished Book Award 2011), were published by Doghouse. He won the Suruga Baika Prize (Japan, 2008) and the Vladimir Devidé Award (Japan, 2012).

Stuart Lane (1932-2007) was from Co. Kildare. He was the founding member of Celbridge writers group. His haiku appeared in *Poetry Ireland Review.*

Leo Lavery was born in Lisburn, Co. Antrim. Educated at Queen's University, Belfast, he worked as a teacher, mostly abroad. He has published two collections of his poems. His haiku appeared in *Blithe Spirit* and elsewhere.

Jessie Lendennie was born in the USA and now lives in Co. Clare. She is a poet and publisher with Salmon Poetry. Her prose poem *Daughter* was first published in 1988. Her haiku appeared on the IHS website. She won the first prize in the *Modern Haiku* competition.

Mark Lonergan is originally from Limerick but now resides on the North side of Dublin. He published his haiku in *The Heron's Nest, Paper Wasp* and *Shamrock*. The latter also published his essays on haiku. He is a member of Haiku Ireland. In 2010, he won the Touchstone Award for an individual haiku.

Seán Lysaght was born in Limerick. At present he lives in Newport, Co. Mayo, and teaches humanities at the Galway-Mayo Institute of Technology, Castlebar. He has published five collections of his poems and translations, the latest being *The Mouth of a River* (Gallery, 2007). His haiku appeared in *Shamrock*.

Aine Mac Aodha is from Omagh, Co. Tyrone. Her collection of poems titled *Where the Three Rivers Meet* was published by Tara Press in 2008. Her haiku appeared in *Shamrock*. She is a member of the IHS.

Seán Mac Mathúna was born in Tralee, Co. Kerry, and now lives in Dublin. He writes in both English and Irish, and has published two collections of short stories, as well as his plays. His haiku appeared in *Lishanu*.

Clare McCotter lives in Co. Derry and works as a psychiatric nurse. Her haiku, tanka and haibun appeared in *Frogpond, Presence, Blithe Spirit, World Haiku Review, Modern Haiku, Simply Haiku*, and *Shamrock*. She is a member of the British Haiku Society. Her debut collection titled *Black Horse Running* was published in 2012. She won the first prize in the IHS haiku competitions 2010 and 2011.

Clare McDonnell is from Co. Donegal. Her collection *Feeling for Infinity* published by Summer Palace Press in 2006 includes some haiku. Her haiku also appeared in *Shamrock* and on the website of the IHS, of which she is a member.

Joe McFadden is a Dubliner and a member of Haiku Ireland. He largely contributed to such editions as *Haiku Spirit* and *Red Thread Haiku* writing articles, book reviews and compiling a haiku bibliography. His haiku appeared on the Haiku Spirit website.

Beth McFarland is from Co. Tyrone, currently based in Germany. Her haiku appeared in *Blithe Spirit, Notes from the Gean, Chrysanthemum* and *Shamrock*. She is a member of the IHS and the British Haiku Society. She won honourable mention in the IHS International Haiku Competition 2011.

Iggy McGovern was born in Coleraine and resides in Dublin, where he is Associate Professor of Physics at Trinity College. He has published two collections of his poetry, the latest being *Safe House* (Dedalus, 2010).

Walter Daniel McGuire is from the south side of Dublin. He published his haiku in *Shamrock* and won honourable mention in the IHS International Haiku Competition 2008. He is a member of the IHS.

Giovanni Malito (1957-2003) was an Italian born in Canada. He later relocated to Cork in Ireland. He wrote poetry, haiku, prose and essays, and edited *The Brobdingnagian Times*, a publication of international poetry. His haiku appeared in *Frogpond, Blithe Spirit* and *The Heron's Nest*.

Michael Massey is from Co. Kilkenny. He has published three collections of his poems. His haiku appeared in *Shamrock*. He is a member of the IHS.

Maire Morrisey-Cummins was born in Tramore, Co. Waterford, and now resides in Co. Wicklow. She is a member of both the IHS and Haiku Ireland, and has poems published on their websites. Her haiku also appeared in *Shamrock*. She won honourable mention in the IHS Haiku Competition 2010.

Joan Newmann was born in Tandragee, Co. Armagh, and now lives in Co. Donegal. She worked as a teacher, and now works as a publisher with Summer Palace Press. She has published five collections, the latest being *Belongings* (Arlen House, 2007; with Kate Newmann). Her haiku have been published in *Shamrock*. She is a member of the IHS.

Kate Newmann is the daughter of Joan Newmann. Born in Co. Down, she lives in Co. Donegal and works as a publisher for Summer Palace Press. She has published three collections, the latest being *Lame Horse* (Arlen House, 2011). Her haiku have been published in *Shamrock*. She is a member of the IHS.

Colette Nic Aodha was born in Shrule, Co. Mayo, and now lives in Galway. A writer in both Irish and English, she has published poetry collections in both languages. Her haiku appeared on the IHS website.

James Norton was born in Dublin where he still lives. In 1995 he founded *Haiku Spirit*, a print Irish journal of haiku and related forms, and was the sole editor of it until 1997. His own haiku appeared in *Hundred Haiku* (Iron Press, 1991) and in various journals such as *Blithe Spirit, Presence, Shamrock* and *Poetry Ireland Review*. His haiku collection titled *Words on the Wind* appeared in 1997 from the Waning Moon Press. He is a member of both Haiku Ireland and the Red Thread Haiku group.

Seán O'Connor is a Dubliner who currently lives in Japan. Between 1998 and 2000 he co-edited *Haiku Spirit* (with James Norton). His haiku appeared there, in *Blithe Spirit* and in *Shamrock*, as well as in *The New Haiku* and *Zen Poems* anthologies. He has published a joint collection of haiku, *Pilgrim Foxes*, with Jim Norton and Ken Jones.

Terry O'Connor is from Galway. He won the Vancouver Cherry Blossom Festival Invitational Haiku Contest 2009. His haiku appeared in *The Heron's Nest, Simply Haiku, Notes from the Gean* and *Shamrock*. He is a member of the IHS.

Tommy Frank O'Connor is from Co. Kerry. He has published a novel, a children's novel, a collection of short stories, a philosophical work and two collections of poetry. His latest collection is *Meeting Mona Lisa* (Doghouse, 2011).

Hugh O'Donnell, a native of Dublin, published his haiku in *Shamrock*. A member of the IHS, he was the winner of the *Shamrock* Readers' Choice Award 2009. He also won honourable mention in the IHS haiku competition 2010. He has published three collections, the most recent being *No Place Like it* (Doghouse, 2010).

Mary O'Donnell, a poet and novelist, was born in Monaghan, and now lives in Maynooth, Co. Kildare. She has published four poetry collections, two novels and a book of short stories. Her haiku appeared in *Shamrock*.

Siofra O'Donovan was born and lives in Co. Wicklow, where she teaches creative writing workshops. She is a novelist, a haiku poet and a founding member of the IHS. In 2006, she worked as writer-in-residence for Co. Louth. She won honourable mention in the Samhain International Haiku Competition 2005.

Dennis O'Driscoll was born in Co. Tipperary and lives in Dublin. He has published five poetry collections. A volume of his *New and Selected Poems* (Anvil) appeared in 2004. He also published literary criticism.

Padraig Ó Horgain is a native of Co. Kerry. His haiku appeared in *Haiku Spirit, Presence* and *Shamrock*, as well as in *The New Haiku* anthology ed. by John Barlow and Martin Lucas.

Mary O'Keeffe is a musician and a music teacher from Co. Cork. A member of the IHS, she published her haiku in *Shamrock*. She was the winner of the IHS International Haiku Competition 2009.

Tom O'Malley was born near Lough Mask, Co. Mayo. He now lives in Co. Meath, and works as a secondary teacher. He has published two collections of poems, the latest being *Journey Backwards* (1998) that has a haiku section.

Cathal Ó Searcaigh is an Irish-language poet born in the Donegal Gaeltacht where he still lives. He has published many collections, some of them bilingual, the latest being *Gleanings* (2006) that includes a few haiku.

Kate (Karen) O'Shea is from Dublin. Her poems have been published in *Acorn*, her haiku in *Shamrock*. She is a member of the IHS.

Maeve O'Sullivan is from Dublin. Her haiku and senryu have appeared in various journals including *Haiku Spirit*, *Blithe Spirit*, *World Haiku Review* and *Shamrock*. Her joint collection of haiku with Kim Richardson, *Double Rainbow*, was published in 2005, followed by her solo collection, *Initial Response* (2011). She is a member of Haiku Ireland and the British Haiku Society.

Ciarán Parkes lives in Galway. He is a poet and founding editor of *Crannóg*, a magazine of poetry. His haiku have been published in *Time Haiku* and in *Shamrock*.

Thomas Powell hails from Wales and is currently living in Co. Armagh. His haiku appeared in *Blithe Spirit*, *Presence*, *Modern Haiku*, *The Heron's Nest* and *Shamrock*. He is a member of the IHS and the British Haiku Society. In 2011, he won the second prize in the IHS Haiku Competition.

Isabelle Prondzynski is from Co. Westmeath, and now divides her time between Belgium and Africa. Her poems have been published in the World Kigo Database and in *Tinywords*. She is a member of the IHS.

Maureen Purcell was born in England of Irish parents, and now lives in Co. Louth. Her haiku have been published in *Shamrock* and in the *Quilt* anthology. She is a member of the IHS.

Justin Quinn was born in Dublin, and now lives in Prague where he lectures in English literature. He was a founding editor of the poetry journal *Metre*, and has published four poetry collections, the latest being *Waves & Trees* (2006).

Mark Roper was born in Derbyshire and lives near Piltown, Co. Kilkenny. He has published four poetry collections, the latest being *Whereabouts* (2005). His haiku have appeared in *Shamrock*. He is a member of the IHS.

Gabriel Rosenstock was born in Kilfinane, Co. Limerick. A poet and essayist, he authored / translated over 100 books, mostly in / into the Irish language. His collection of haiku titled *Cold Moon: Erotic Haiku* appeared in 1993. A collection of his newer haiku, *Where Light Begins*, came out in 2012. His two books of essays on haiku, *Haiku Enlightenment* and *Haiku, the Gentle Art of Disappearing* were published in 2009.

John W. Sexton was born in England and now lives in Co. Kerry. His collection of haiku titled *Shadows Bloom / Scáthanna Faoi Bhláth* with translations into Irish by Gabriel Rosenstock was published by Doghouse in 2004. His newer haiku appeared in *Modern Haiku, Frogpond, The Heron's Nest* and *Shamrock*. He also published four collections of his mainstream poems and his fiction. His fifth collection of poems is forthcoming from Salmon Poetry in 2012.

John Sheahan, a Dubliner, is a musician with the legendary band "The Dubliners". His haiku appeared in *Shamrock*.

Eileen Sheehan lives in Killarney, Co Kerry. She has published two collections with Doghouse, the latest being *Down the Sunlit Hall* (2008). Her haiku appeared in *Acorn, The Heron's Nest, Haiku Scotland, Frogpond* and *Shamrock*.

Breid Sibley lives in Co. Galway. Her haiku have been published in *Shamrock*. She is a member of the IHS and the Baffle poetry group.

Bee Smith was born in the USA and now lives in Co. Cavan. Her poems have been published in *World Haiku Review* and in *Shamrock*. She is a member of the IHS.

Martin Vaughan was born in Tipperary and lives in Dublin. A co-founder and a member of the Board of the IHS, he has published his haiku in *Shamrock* and on the World Kigo Database (Japan). He was a runner-up in the *Shamrock* Readers' Choice Award 2008.

Aisling White is from North Co. Dublin. A member of the Board of the IHS, she has published her haiku in *Shamrock* and on the World Kigo Database (Japan). She was a runner-up in the *Shamrock* Readers' Choice Award 2009.

Also available from DOGHOUSE:

Every DOGHOUSE book costs €12, postage free, to anywhere
in the world (& other known planets). Cheques, Postal Orders
(or any legal method) payable to DOGHOUSE, also PAYPAL
(www.paypal.com) to doghousepaypal@eircom.net

*"Buy a full set of DOGHOUSE books, in time they will be
collectors' items"* - Gabriel Fitzmaurice, April 12, 2005.
DOGHOUSE
P.O. Box 312
Tralee G.P.O.
Tralee
Co. Kerry
Ireland
tel + 353 6671 37547
email doghouse312@eircom.net
www.doghousebooks.ie